for Prism
Premiered November 19, 2004 at Symphony Space, New Yo...

Scherzino

Soprano Saxophone in B♭

WILLIAM BOLCOM
2004

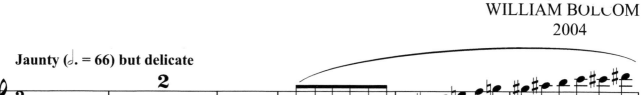

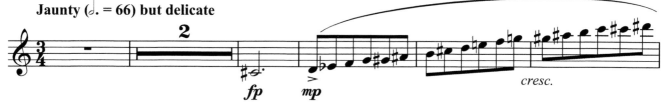

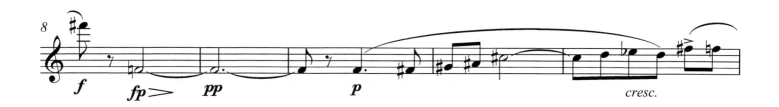

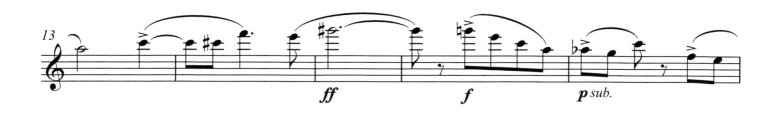

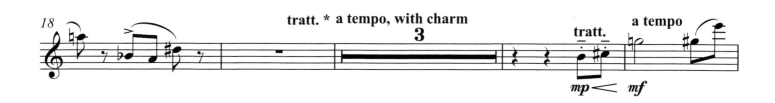

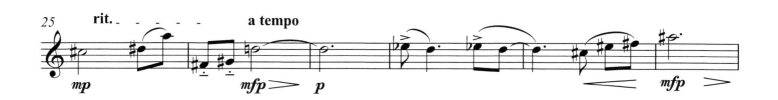

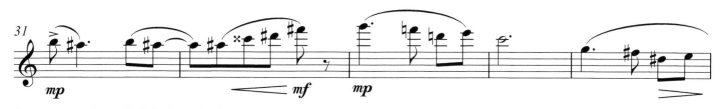

*trattenuto = just slightly held back

Scherzino

WILLIAM BOLCOM

Soprano Saxophone in B♭

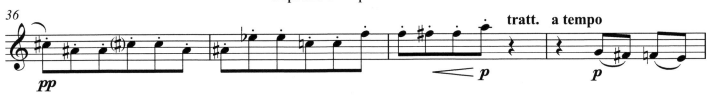

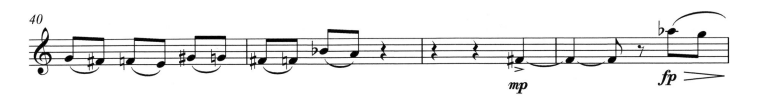

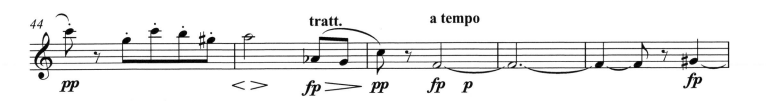

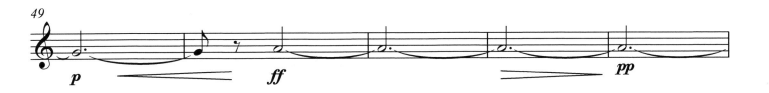

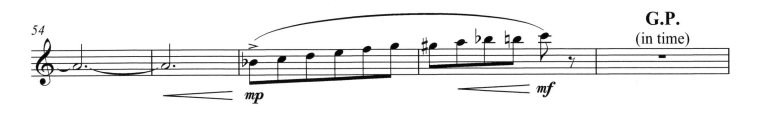

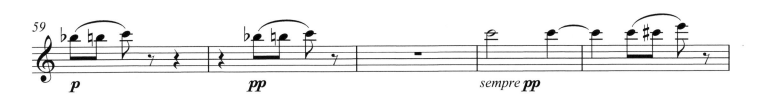

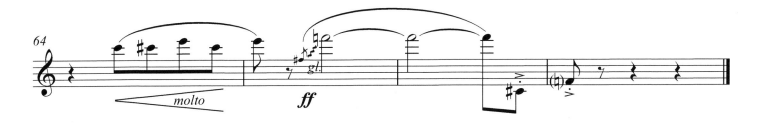